Express Aisle

Gourmet

RECIPES PREPARED WITH 12 ITEMS OR LESS!

Introduction

I wrote this book for home chefs who enjoy preparing tasty meals but are either plagued by the angst of failure, or simply pressed for time.

Over the past several years I've noticed supermarkets carrying a variety of fresh, pre-cut vegetables. In addition, some supermarkets have butcher departments with restaurant-style cuts of meat, expansive fresh seafood selections, and an ever-increasing array of items that are typically used by chefs in professional kitchens, such as demi-glace, high quality oils & vinegars, and more.

This book is full of restaurant quality recipes that can be made at home using ingredients that either are simple to prepare or that can be purchased pre-prepared from the grocery store. (Think pre-diced onions, sliced carrots, chicken broth, etc...).

Keeping in mind that fresh, seasonal ingredients are the basic fundamentals of cooking; I developed these recipes in my own kitchen. I have also included a list of pantry and refrigerator items that are helpful to have on hand and a list of basic cooking equipment and utensils that should be found in all kitchens.

Cooking Technique

The foundation of every good chef is his *mise en place* (things in place). All chefs prepare and assemble the ingredients that will go into a recipe before they embark on the process of actually cooking. Since the most laborious and often longest part of a meal is the preparation, once complete, the cooking is a cinch.

Preparation is where the grocery store comes in handy. While each recipe in this book is written as if you are going to prepare everything from scratch, if you are pressed for time look for those recipe ingredients that can be purchased pre-prepared from the store.

Once preparation is complete, it is time to pre-heat the oven or start the flame. Cooking is largely about common sense and basic principles. "Season main ingredient, heat pan, add oil, add ingredients, turn, cook until desired doneness and serve." Once you get the fundamentals down you can cook anything.

Seasoning

You must remember to season. Frequently, this vital step is forgotten. In most cases, proper seasoning is the difference between serving a great meal that will be fondly remembered and a meal that is bland and not memorable at all. Seasoning means salt & pepper. It has nothing to do with herbs or spices. Seasoning is not a one shot thing. All the elements in the dish must be seasoned. Seasoning occurs at the beginning and throughout the cooking process, not at the end. Seasoning only at the end makes for a salty dish.

Timing

As with any recipe, cooking times are based on the size and type of item that is being cooked. Typically, fish cooks faster than chicken. Chicken cooks faster than steak, and vegetables cook very fast. Don't be afraid to cook on high heat. When you put ingredients in the pan leave them alone to cook. Excessive stirring is usually not necessary. Lower the heat if ingredients become too hot and start to burn. Don't be afraid of smoke or flame. Don't be afraid of experimenting. And most importantly, don't be afraid of making a mistake. We usually learn the most when we make mistakes.

Now it is up to you. Let the recipes in this book offer inspiration, let nature, farmers, and the supermarket provide quality ingredients. Create a guest list of your favorite people and get into the kitchen and start cooking!

Most of the recipes in this book serve 2 people.

Author Bio

Bill Dertouzos is a graduate of the Culinary Institute of America, former chef at the Maui Grand Wailea Hotel, and executive chef at the award-winning Pangaea Restaurant at the Hotel Nikko Beverly Hills, CA. His current ventures, Flatbush and J Gourmet Co. Inc., provide catering services for corporate and executive clientele.

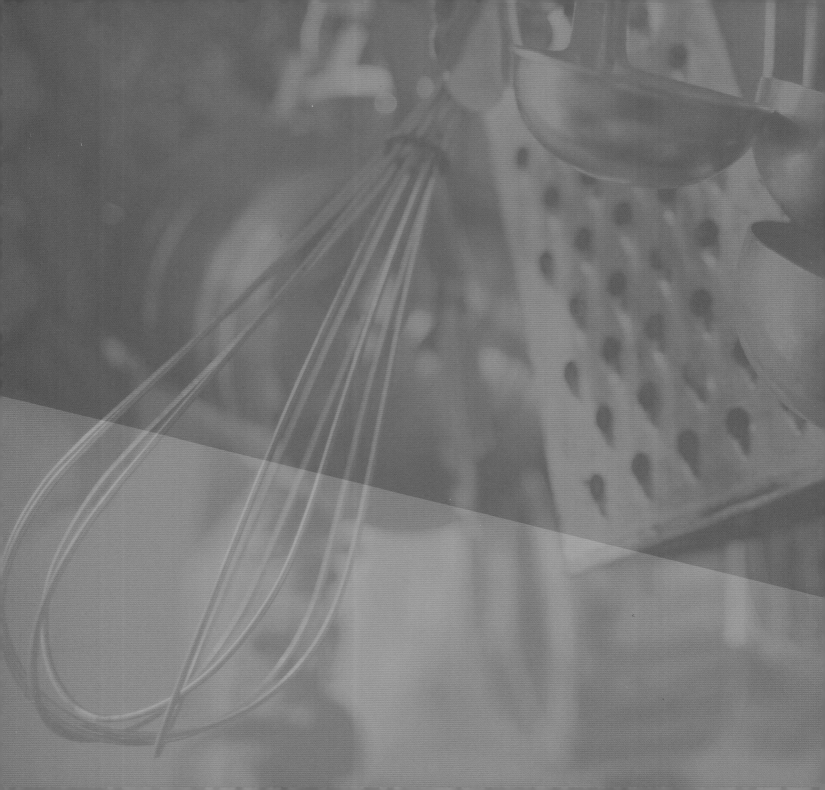

Contents

Breakfast

Almost Eggs Florentine

Making classic egg dishes at home can be a daunting challenge. This Eggs Florentine recipe is simple and delicious. Try it for yourself and overcome any fear you've had about serving fancy eggs at home.

Heat butter in a medium skillet. Add garlic and sauté until it gives off a nice aroma. Add spinach and toss with tongs until wilted—about 2 minutes. Add cream, turn heat to high, bring to a rapid boil, and reduce to a thick consistency—this should take about 5 minutes, being careful not to burn. Add nutmeg and cheese, and season with salt and pepper. Set aside.

Fill a small skillet ⅓ full with water. Add vinegar and bring to a boil. Reduce to medium-high heat and gently break the eggs into the water. After a minute, nudge the eggs with a slotted spoon to keep them from sticking then gently flip over and poach until desired doneness.

Toast English muffins while the eggs are cooking.

To serve, place an English muffin onto each plate. Top each muffin half with 2 tomato slices, spinach, and one egg.

TIP: Vinegar plays a vital role in this dish as the acids assist the cooking process and hold the eggs together.

1 tbs butter

1 tbs minced garlic

½ lb baby spinach

1 cup heavy cream

Pinch of nutmeg

2 tbs shredded Swiss or Gruyère cheese

2 tbs white vinegar

4 eggs

2 English muffins

8 thin tomato slices

Kosher salt & freshly ground pepper

The Indiscriminate Frittata

Don't get too caught up on the measurements with this dish. By design, it is meant to utilize items that have been in the refrigerator for a while. Refrain from adding tomatoes—they will make the frittata runny. Fresh herbs also are a good addition.

Pre-heat oven to 325°F.

Heat oil and butter in a medium skillet. Add potato, onions, peppers, and zucchini. Add any extra items from your refrigerator (e.g.: bacon, sausage, ham, chicken). Cook until the vegetables begin to soften then season with salt and pepper.

Whisk eggs in a large bowl, then add to the skillet. Stir until combined. Once eggs begin to set, transfer the skillet to the oven for 15–20 minutes. The frittata is done when the center is firm. Sprinkle cheese over the top and return to the oven until it melts; about 5 minutes.

Slice the frittata like a pie and serve on a plate alone, with a salad, or sliced fruit.

1 tsp canola oil

1 tsp butter

1 lb diced potatoes

½ cup chopped onions

¼ cup diced red bell peppers

½ cup sliced zucchini

8 eggs

⅓ cup grated cheddar cheese

Kosher salt & freshly ground pepper

Scrambled Eggs and Fettuccine

I first saw this dish about 20 years ago and liked the combination of eggs and pasta. It makes for a filling breakfast when you need a little extra sustenance in the morning.

Cook pasta in a large pot of boiling, salted water according to package instructions. Rinse under cool water, drain, and set aside.

Heat oil in a medium skillet. Cut sausages into 1 inch pieces and brown in the skillet for about 5 minutes, then add onions and mushrooms. Cook until onions are translucent and mushrooms have a little color, about 5 minutes. Crack eggs into a small bowl and whisk until combined then pour into the skillet. Stir until eggs are cooked to desired consistency. Add pasta, mix together, and season to taste with salt and pepper.

Serve Scrambled Eggs and Fettuccine in pasta bowls. If desired, sprinkle with chopped parsley, diced tomato, shredded cheese, and a dash of Tabasco®.

9 oz fresh fettuccine

1 tbs canola oil

8 oz link sausages

½ cup diced onions

1 cup sliced mushrooms

4 eggs

Kosher salt & freshly ground pepper

Healthy Joes

For those health conscious people who still crave a hearty breakfast, the Healthy Joe will surely satisfy. Unlike its brother, the Sloppy Joe, the Healthy Joe is prepared with egg whites and lean chicken, which make it a healthier choice.

Pre-heat oven to 300°F.

Heat oil in a medium ovenproof skillet. Add peppers, onions, garlic, and chicken. Use a wooden spoon to break chicken apart and cook until browned. Add spinach and wilt, about 1 minute. Add egg whites and tomatoes. Sprinkle cheese over the top and place skillet in the oven until cheese melts—about 5 minutes.

Serve Healthy Joes in bowls over rice or with a warm onion roll.

1 tbs canola oil

¼ cup diced bell peppers

½ cup diced onions

1 tbs minced garlic

1 lb ground chicken

16 oz baby spinach

6 oz egg whites

1 cup diced tomatoes

¼ cup grated cheddar cheese

Fried Eggs with Corned Beef Hash

When I first learned how to make this recipe I was stunned by how good corned beef hash could be. The key is using quality ingredients. Once you've prepared this dish my way, you will be hard pressed to return to canned hash.

Heat oil in a medium skillet. Add celery, onions, and peppers, then reduce heat to medium. Add potatoes, 1 tablespoon butter, corned beef, mustard powder, and chili powder. Cook for 5–7 minutes until corned beef is heated through.

Melt remaining butter in a small skillet to coat the bottom. Crack eggs into the pan two at a time and fry until over easy.

Divide hash onto two plates and serve with eggs on the side.

1 tbs canola oil

¼ cup diced celery

½ cup diced onions

¼ cup diced bell peppers

1 cup diced potatoes

2 tsp butter, separated

¾ lb corned beef cubed into ½ inch pieces

1 tsp mustard powder

¼ tsp chili powder

1 tbs butter

4 eggs

The Ultimate French Toast

This variation of simple French toast will surely knock your socks off. Nutella® is not very well known in the United States, but the Italians sure figured out how to take peanut butter to the next level.

Pre-heat oven to 325°F.

Spread Nutella® liberally on 2 slices of bread and close like a sandwich. Whisk eggs, milk, vanilla, nutmeg, and cinnamon in a medium bowl. Soak bread in egg mixture, liberally on both sides.

Melt butter in a medium skillet then add bread and reduce heat to medium low. Once the side is golden brown, flip and cook until golden (2–3 minutes) on the other side. Place on a rimmed baking sheet and bake in the oven for about 5 minutes.

Slice bread on a diagonal. Stack 1 piece on top of the other at an angle. Spoon fruit over the top and sprinkle with powdered sugar. If desired, pour a little maple syrup around the border.

1 jar Nutella®

4 thick slices of bread (challa, Hawaiian sweet bread, brioche, etc...)

4 eggs

½ cup whole milk

1 tsp vanilla

Pinch of nutmeg

Pinch of cinnamon

1 tbs butter

¾ cup assorted berries (strawberries, blueberries)

Powdered sugar

Maple syrup

Pasta

Aunt Becky's Spaghetti

Being of Greek descent, this dish has a certain place in my heart. My favorite aunt, Becky, made this better than anyone I know, including me. You'll be surprised how 4 simple ingredients can add up to a perfect meal.

Cook spaghetti in a large pot of boiling, salted water according to package instructions. Drain, and set aside.

Melt butter in a medium skillet until it browns then add lemon juice (this will stop the butter from burning), Parmagiano-Reggiano, and pasta. Toss together and season to taste with salt and pepper.

Divide spaghetti into 2 pasta bowls and garnish with Parmagiano-Reggiano. If desired, sprinkle with chopped basil, tarragon, and lemon zest (or other fresh herbs).

16 oz spaghetti

½ cup butter

1 tsp fresh lemon juice

¼ cup freshly grated Parmagiano-Reggiano

Kosher salt & freshly ground pepper

Mediterranean Fusilli

No cream, no butter, and no meat make this dish a light and healthy vegetarian meal. It tastes just as good, if not better, cold the next day. It is also the perfect dish to make ahead and bring to a picnic.

Cook fusilli in a large pot of boiling, salted water according to package instructions. Drain, and set aside.

Heat oil in a medium skillet. Add onions and sauté until translucent then add tomatoes and wine and reduce by half. Add olives and chicken broth and bring to a boil. Remove from heat and add thyme, olive oil, pasta, and feta. Toss all ingredients until combined and season with salt and pepper.

Divide fusilli into 2 pasta bowls and garnish with fresh thyme leaves. If desired, sprinkle toasted pine nuts on top.

1 cup fusilli pasta

1 tbs canola oil

¼ cup diced red onions

½ cup cherry tomatoes cut in half

¼ cup white wine

¼ cup pitted Kalamata olives

¼ cup chicken broth

2 tbs fresh whole thyme leaves

¼ cup extra virgin olive oil

½ cup cubed feta cheese

Kosher salt & freshly ground pepper

Angel Hair Primavera

This dish was wildly popular in the early 80's and one of the first I learned. Like The Indiscriminate Frittata, it is great for utilizing leftover ingredients. In my opinion, the garlic and the cheese are what bring this pasta alive. Feel free to add any extra vegetables that are in your refrigerator.

Cook pasta in a large pot of boiling, salted water according to package instructions. Drain, and set aside.

Heat canola oil in a medium skillet. Add onions, peppers, squash, and garlic (and any other vegetables that you might be using). Stir. Remove from heat and add olive oil, Parmagiano-Reggiano, basil, and pasta. Season with salt and pepper and toss until well combined.

Divide Angel Hair Primavera into 2 deep bowls and garnish with Parmagiano-Reggiano. Sprinkle with additional chopped basil.

9 oz fresh angel hair pasta

1 tbs canola oil

½ cup diced onions

¼ cup diced bell peppers

1 cup diced squash

1 tbs minced garlic

¼ cup extra virgin olive oil

¼ cup freshly grated Parmagiano-Reggiano

1 tbs chopped basil

Kosher salt & freshly ground pepper

Fettuccine Alfredo with Rock Shrimp

Whenever I show people how to make this they are stunned by its simplicity. There is no mystery or magic—just watch the egg yolk technique and you'll have a fantastic dish with little effort.

Cook fettuccine in a large pot of boiling, salted water according to package instructions. Drain, and set aside.

Heat oil in a medium skillet. Add rock shrimp and season with salt and pepper. Cook for about 2 minutes then add cream and reduce by $\frac{1}{3}$. (It is ok if it starts to boil, just stir). Remove from heat and prepare for the tricky part. Whisk egg yolk into the cream (do this very quickly or you will end up with scrambled eggs) then whisk in Parmagiano-Reggiano and pasta. Season to taste with salt and pepper, tossing until all ingredients are combined.

Divide fettuccine into 2 pasta bowls and garnish with Parmagiano-Reggiano. If desired, sprinkle with diced tomatoes and chopped parsley.

9 oz fresh fettuccine

1 tbs canola oil

¾ lb rock shrimp

1½ cups heavy cream

1 egg yolk

¼ cup freshly grated Parmagiano-Reggiano

Kosher salt & freshly ground pepper

Linguine with Clam Sauce

Every Brooklynite thinks their recipe for this dish is the best. I know mine is supreme. There is no magic. Master this recipe and join the rest of us by claiming that your Linguini with Clam Sauce is the best.

Cook linguine in a large pot of boiling, salted water according to package instructions. Drain, and set aside.

Rinse clams in fresh water removing any sand. Heat canola oil in a large skillet. Add onions and garlic and sauté until translucent. Add clams, wine, and clam juice or stock. Cover, lower the heat, and simmer for 5 minutes. Remove clams as they begin to open. Once all clams are open, reduce the cooking liquid, stir in butter, and add pasta. Gently toss all ingredients until combined and season with salt and pepper. Discard clams that don't open.

Divide linguine into 2 pasta bowls. Arrange clams on top, drizzle with olive oil and sprinkle with Parmagiano-Reggiano. If desired, garnish with chopped parsley.

9 oz fresh linguine

2 lbs clams, the smaller the better, manila or cherrystone

1 tbs canola oil

¼ cup diced onions

1 tbs minced garlic

½ cup white wine

¼ cup clam juice or fish stock

1 tbs butter

1 tsp freshly grated Parmagiano-Reggiano

Drizzle of extra virgin olive oil

Kosher salt & freshly ground pepper

Fettuccine with Salmon-Cream Sauce

This recipe brings back memories of living in Greenwich Village. There was a little café down a back street alley that served it. Use the best caviar that you can find.

Cook fettuccine in a large pot of boiling, salted water according to package instructions. Drain, and set aside.

Heat oil in a medium skillet. Add onions and sauté for 3–5 minutes until translucent. Add vodka—it will ignite—and let the alcohol burn off, then add cream and dill, and reduce by ⅓. Add salmon, caviar, and pasta. Toss all ingredients until combined and season with salt and pepper.

Divide fettuccine into 2 pasta bowls and garnish with Parmagiano-Reggiano and dill sprigs.

9 oz fresh fettuccine

1 tbs canola oil

½ cup diced onions

¼ cup vodka

1½ cups heavy cream

1 tbs chopped fresh dill

4 oz smoked salmon

1 tbs caviar

1 tsp freshly grated
Parmagiano-Reggiano

Kosher salt & freshly ground pepper

Spinach with Fettuccine

This was one of the first dishes I learned in my cooking career. I thought I was "Escoffier" because it was so good. The sweetness of the Marsala combined with the richness of the cream make it a bit of heaven on earth.

Cook fettuccine in a large pot of boiling, salted water according to package instructions. Drain, and set aside.

Heat oil in a medium skillet. Add spinach and wilt for 1 minute then add Marsala and reduce by half. Add cream, demi-glace, Parmagiano-Reggiano, and pasta. Toss all ingredients until combined and season with salt and pepper.

Divide fettuccine into 2 pasta bowls and garnish with Parmagiano-Reggiano. If desired, add a few diced tomatoes on the top.

9 oz fresh fettuccine

1 tbs canola oil

1 cup baby spinach

¼ cup Marsala wine

1½ cups heavy cream

1 tsp veal demi-glace

¼ cup freshly grated Parmagiano-Reggiano

Kosher salt & freshly ground pepper

Eggplant and Smoked Mozzarella Rigatoni

This recipe comes from my good friend, Jeff Moogk, by way of San Diego. The combination of ingredients and flavors marry well. As always, fresh, top quality ingredients make for the best results.

Cook rigatoni in a large pot of boiling, salted water according to package instructions. Drain, and set aside.

Heat oil in a medium skillet. Add eggplant and brown on all sides. If the pan becomes dry, add more oil. Once eggplant is evenly browned, add tomatoes and garlic and toss. Add wine and reduce for 1–2 minutes. Add mozzarella, basil, and pasta. Toss all ingredients until combined and season with salt and pepper.

Divide rigatoni into 2 pasta bowls. Garnish with chopped fresh basil and Parmagiano-Reggiano.

1 cup rigatoni

2 tbs canola oil

2/3 cup eggplant, diced into 1/2 inch cubes

1 cup diced Roma tomatoes

1 tbs minced garlic

1/4 cup white wine

1/2 cup diced smoked mozzarella

1/4 cup fresh chopped basil

Kosher salt & freshly ground pepper

Pasta Pomodoro

My book would not be complete without including the most basic of pasta dishes, Pasta Pomodoro, a true classic that is enjoyed by all. If you have never made pasta in your life, this is the perfect starting place.

Cook linguine in a large pot of boiling, salted water according to package instructions. Drain, and set aside.

Heat canola oil in a medium skillet. Add tomatoes, garlic, wine, basil, and olive oil. Remove from heat and add pasta and Parmagiano-Reggiano. Toss ingredients until combined and season with salt and pepper.

Divide linguine into 2 pasta bowls and garnish with Parmagiano-Reggiano and fresh basil.

9 oz fresh linguine or spaghetti

1 tbs canola oil

2 cups diced Roma tomatoes

1 tbs minced garlic

¼ cup white wine

¼ cup fresh chopped basil

¼ cup extra virgin olive oil

¼ cup freshly grated Parmagiano-Reggiano

Kosher salt & freshly ground pepper

Open-Faced Ravioli

This dish is a little challenging to make, but looks impressive on a plate. The classic combination of mushrooms, leeks, chicken, cream, and butter makes for a rich meal. Serve at a dinner party and your guests will surely be impressed.

Cook lasagna in a large pot of boiling, salted water according to package instructions. Drain, and set aside.

Heat oil in a medium skillet. Add chicken and cook for 2 minutes on each side. Remove, cover, and set aside.

Pour grease out and place skillet over medium-high heat. Add mushrooms, leeks, and garlic, stir, and season with salt and pepper. Add wine and de-glaze the skillet using a wooden spoon. Reduce by half then add chicken broth. Return chicken to the skillet and reduce heat to medium. Cover, and cook for 5 minutes. Turn chicken over and cook for 10 more minutes. Add demi-glace, cream, and butter.

To serve, place 1 sheet of lasagna on each plate. Place chicken diagonally on top of the pasta—corner to corner. Spoon half of the sauce over the chicken. Place the second lasagna sheet on top of the chicken, folding back one corner. Pour remaining sauce over the top.

9 oz fresh lasagna sheets

1 tbs canola oil

2– 6 oz boneless, skinless chicken breasts

½ cup sliced mushrooms

¼ cup diced leeks, white part only

1 tsp minced garlic

¼ cup white wine

2 cups chicken broth

¼ cup veal demi-glace

¼ cup of heavy cream

1 tsp butter

Kosher salt & freshly ground pepper

Tortellini with Gorgonzola and Pine Nuts

This is one of the first pastas I learned. It was one of our "simple specials" for the evening, and I thought I was king salami. It's a strongly flavored dish, and worthy of that good bottle of red wine you've been saving.

Cook tortellini in a large pot of boiling, salted water according to package instructions. Drain, and set aside.

Add cream to the same pot and reduce by ⅓ over high heat. Remove pot from heat, add Gorgonzola, and whip until smooth. Add pine nuts and tortellini. Toss all ingredients until combined and season with salt and pepper.

Divide tortellini into 2 pasta bowls and sprinkle Parmagiano-Reggiano and fresh parsley over the top.

9 oz fresh tortellini

1½ cups heavy cream

½ cup crumbled Gorgonzola cheese

¼ cup pine nuts

1 tsp freshly grated Parmagiano-Reggiano

1 tsp parsley

Kosher salt & freshly ground pepper

Spaghetti Bolognese

There are many ways to make a Bolognese sauce. This may be the easiest and will stand up to the best of them. It's hearty and flavorful and tastes great the next day. Feel free to substitute the combinations of beef, pork, and lamb or just use all beef.

Heat canola oil in a stock pot. Once the oil is hot, add onions and garlic. Stir in wine and reduce by half. Add pork, and beef, and season generously with salt and pepper. Using a wooden spoon, break the meat into small pieces as it browns. Once the meat is evenly brown, add tomatoes (including liquid). Lower the heat and simmer for about 40 minutes. Add Parmagiano-Reggiano and adjust seasoning to taste.

Meanwhile, cook spaghetti in a large pot of boiling, salted water according to package instructions. Drain, and set aside.

Divide spaghetti into 2 pasta bowls. Liberally spoon the sauce over the top. Drizzle with olive oil and sprinkle with more Parmagiano-Reggiano.

1 tbs canola oil

½ cup diced onions

1 tbs minced garlic

¼ cup red wine

16 oz ground pork

8 oz ground beef

14.5 oz can diced tomatoes

28 oz can crushed tomatoes

¼ cup freshly grated Parmagiano-Reggiano

9 oz fresh spaghetti

Drizzle of extra virgin olive oil

Kosher salt & freshly ground pepper

Seafood

Fish en Papillote

Direct translation = fish in parchment paper. When done right this dish is very impressive. You'll get lots of oohhs and aahhs around the dinner table. The fish is cooked and served in the parchment. When the bag is cut open, there's steam, aroma, and a beautifully cooked piece of fish.

Pre-heat oven to 325°F.

Heat oil in a medium skillet, add leeks and garlic and stir 1–2 minutes. Add vermouth and cream and reduce by ⅓.

Place ½ of the cream mixture onto one side of each piece of parchment. (You'll be folding the other ½ over the top). Place fish on top of the mixture. Season with salt and pepper and place a sprig or two of the herb on top. Add lemon wedges, olives, and garlic cloves, then fold and roll the edges of the parchment to seal tightly. Rub a small amount of oil on the top of the paper to protect it from burning. Place both parchment packages on a rimmed sheet pan and bake in the oven for about 8 minutes.

Remove from the oven and place one parchment bag in the middle of each plate. Tear it open and enjoy.

1 tbs canola oil

½ cup diced leeks, white parts only

1 minced garlic clove

2 tbs dry vermouth

¼ cup heavy cream

2—8 oz firm fish filets
(e.g.: halibut, salmon, sole)

4 tarragon, dill, or thyme sprigs

4 lemon wedges

4 green olives with pimentos,
thinly sliced

4–6 garlic cloves, crushed but
not peeled

Kosher salt & freshly ground pepper

2 sheets parchment paper, cut to
16" square

Salmon with Avocado and Mango Salsa

Not only is this a great dish, it's a fresh and satisfying meal. The combination of ingredients work so well together, and all you need to do is dice fruit and cook the salmon.

Pre-heat oven to 300°F.

Season salmon on both sides with salt and pepper. Heat canola oil in an ovenproof skillet. Add salmon and cook on each side for 2 minutes. Place skillet in the oven and bake for 6–7 minutes.

In a large bowl combine mangoes, onions, and avocado. Season to taste with salt and pepper, drizzle with balsamic vinegar and olive oil, and toss well.

Divide salmon on two plates and place a scoop of Mango Salsa over the top.

2—6 oz salmon filets

1 tbs canola oil

1 cup mango chunks (canned or fresh)

½ cup diced red onions

1 ripe avocado, diced

2 tbs balsamic vinegar (fig balsamic vinegar is my favorite)

¼ cup extra virgin olive oil

Kosher salt & freshly ground pepper

Seafood Paella

This is a quick and tasty variation for the national dish of Spain. Unlike traditional paella this recipe is ready to serve in a fraction of the time. All of the classic elements are here except the Arborio rice is substituted with orzo.

Season chicken with salt and pepper. Clean clams, mussels, and shrimp.

Cook orzo in a large pot of boiling, salted water according to package instructions. Drain, and set aside.

Heat oil in a large pot. Add chicken and brown on all sides, then add the onions, tomatoes, peas, clams, mussels, shrimp, sherry, garlic, and broth. Stir, then cover and reduce heat to medium and cook for 10 minutes. Uncover and stir in orzo and saffron and season. Once the clams and mussels have opened, the paella is done. Discard any unopened clams and mussels.

Divide paella into 2 deep bowls to serve.

8 oz chicken pieces

4 clams

4–5 mussels

6 large shrimp

1 cup dried orzo

1 tbs canola oil

½ cup diced onions

¼ cup diced tomatoes

½ cup peas

¼ cup sherry

1 tbs minced garlic

1 cup chicken broth

1–2 saffron threads

Kosher salt & freshly ground pepper

Lemon wedges

Halibut, Heirloom Tomatoes, and Ravioli

While perfecting the art of canning heirloom tomatoes, this recipe was created. I found myself with a few extra tomatoes, some halibut, and ravioli in the refrigerator. It was time for dinner, I was hungry, so voilà! This recipe was born. Enjoy!

Pre-heat oven to 300°F.

Cook ravioli in a large pot of boiling, salted water according to package instructions. Drain, and set aside.

Rinse and remove stems from tomatoes, place on a rimmed sheet pan, and generously season with salt and pepper. Add enough olive oil to thoroughly coat and bake in the oven until they're really soft—about 20 minutes. Remove and chop coarsely. (There will be a lot of liquid).

Season halibut with salt and pepper. Heat canola oil in a large skillet. Add halibut and cook 3—5 minutes per side until done. Add garlic and tomatoes to the skillet, season with salt and pepper, and add basil.

To serve, arrange tomatoes in the center of 2 plates. Place halibut on top and ravioli around the sides. Drizzle a little olive oil around the plates and garnish with fresh basil.

1—9 oz package cheese ravioli

2 large heirloom tomatoes

Extra virgin olive oil

2—6 oz halibut filets

1 tbs canola oil

1 tsp minced garlic

3 large basil leaves, coarsely chopped

Kosher salt & freshly ground pepper

Black Mussels with Sausage

If you are going to make mussels, make them this way. The combination of sausage, cream, and vermouth create an unparalleled flavor sensation.

Cut sausage into half lengthwise, then half again. Cut the strips into a ¼ inch dice. Heat oil in a stock pot. Add sausage and cook for 2 minutes then add onions. Once onions begin to caramelize, add vermouth to deglaze the pan. (Don't worry if it flames, the alcohol will burn off quickly). Add mussels and cream. Toss everything together, cover, and cook for 5 minutes or less. When mussels start to open, they're done. Discard mussels that don't open.

Serve mussels in their broth in deep bowls with a chunk of crusty bread on the side. If desired, garnish with chopped parsley and diced tomatoes.

1 lb Louisiana hot sausages

1 tbs canola oil

¼ cup diced red onion

½ cup dry vermouth

1½ to 2 lbs black lip mussels

¾ cup heavy cream

Sautéed Salmon with Squash

What makes this dish unique is serving it with the Crispy Noodle Cake (recipe p. 111) rather than over pasta. It's a variation on the crispy noodles in Chinese restaurants; only more refined. While other types of fish can be substituted, I believe that salmon is the best choice.

Pre-heat oven to 325°F.

Season salmon on both sides with salt and pepper. Heat 1 tablespoon of oil in an oven-proof pan. Add salmon and cook on each side for 2 minutes then bake in the oven for about 6–7 minutes, until done.

Heat remaining oil and butter in a medium skillet. Add squash and season with salt and pepper. Just before it's done, add basil and toss. Be careful not to overcook the squash— it doesn't take long.

To serve, cut Crispy Noodle Cake into 4 pieces and place 2 pieces on each plate—tips pointing outward. Arrange salmon on top and squash on the side. Serve with a dollop of tartar sauce if desired.

2—6 oz salmon filets

2 tbs canola oil, separated

1 tsp butter

1 cup sliced yellow squash

2 tbs chopped basil

Kosher salt & freshly ground pepper

Sautéed Halibut with Orzo

Escolar was the fish I originally used for this recipe. Now, I substitute other whitefish. This entrée was a top seller at one of my restaurants. It's a full flavored Mediterranean style dish. To take it to the next level, use Pernod instead of white wine.

Cook orzo in a large pot of boiling, salted water according to package instructions. Drain, and set aside.

Season fish on all sides with salt and pepper. Heat oil in a large skillet. Add halibut and cook for 1 minute on each side. Remove, and set aside.

In the same skillet, add leeks and sauté. Add wine, deglaze the pan, reduce by half, and then add chicken broth. Return fish to the skillet and reduce heat to simmer. When fish is done, remove, cover with foil, and set aside. Reduce poaching liquid by ⅓. Swirl in 1 tablespoon of butter and season with salt and pepper. Set aside.

Melt remaining butter in a large skillet and add cooked orzo. Season with salt and pepper, add thyme, and heat thoroughly. Add cheese and olives, and stir.

To serve, spoon orzo into the center of plates. Arrange fish over the top and drizzle with sauce. Garnish with lemon zest and chopped mint.

If desired, substitute ingredients such as fennel, shiitake mushrooms, red onions, and artichoke hearts to add variety to this dish.

4 oz dried orzo

2—6 oz halibut filets, cubed

1 tbs canola oil

½ cup diced leeks
(white parts only)

¼ cup dry white wine

1 cup chicken broth

2 tbs butter, separated

½ tsp chopped thyme

Lemon zest

3 oz goat or feta cheese

2 tbs sliced kalamata olives

1 tomato, seeded and chopped

Kosher salt & freshly ground pepper

Fresh mint

Shrimp and Scallop Risotto

The risotto is what makes this dish special. The shrimp and scallops are merely the supporting cast. I like to make the risotto first, then the shrimp and scallops.

Prepare risotto (recipe p. 108).

Rinse shrimp and scallops with cold water and pat dry. Heat oil in a large skillet and add shrimp, scallops, and wine. Reduce by half, then add cream and reduce by ⅓. Top with butter and season with salt and pepper as butter melts. Add risotto and season. Garnish with chopped chives and serve.

10 medium shrimp, peeled and de-veined

4 large scallops

1 tbs canola oil

½ cup white wine

½ cup heavy cream

1 tsp butter

Kosher salt & freshly ground pepper

Chives

Salmon with Succotash

"Sufferin' salmon succotash" I hear Yosemite Sam say when I prepare this meal in the summertime. Succotash is a delicious combination of vegetables. Try to use wild salmon if possible or substitute salmon with other fish if desired.

Pre-heat oven to 325°F.

Season salmon on both sides with salt and pepper. Heat oil in a large, ovenproof skillet. Add salmon and cook on each side for 2 minutes then bake in the oven for about 6–7 minutes, until done.

While salmon is cooking, melt butter in a medium skillet. Add onions and peppers, stirring. When onions begin turning transparent about 5 minutes, add corn and season with salt and pepper. Add sage, beans, and wine. Reduce heat to medium, add cream, season again, and stir.

Remove salmon from the oven and arrange it on two plates. Serve succotash on top of the fish and if desired, drizzle with maple syrup. Rice Pilaf (recipe p. 110) is a complementary side dish.

2—6 oz salmon filets

1 tbs canola oil

1 tbs butter

½ cup diced red onions

¼ cup diced bell peppers

1 cup frozen corn

1 tsp fresh chopped sage

½ cup lima or fava beans

¼ cup white wine

1 tbs heavy cream

Drizzle of maple syrup (optional)

Kosher salt & freshly ground pepper

Shrimp in a Black Bean Sauce

This is one of those all-time Chinese favorites. Use big, plump shrimp and your finished product will rival your local Chinese restaurant's.

Rinse shrimp in cold water and pat dry. Heat oil in a large skillet. Add shrimp, onions, peppers, garlic, ginger, wine, black bean sauce, and broth. In a small bowl, mix together soy sauce and cornstarch then add to the skillet. Reduce to low and cook until shrimp are pink, stirring occasionally while the sauce thickens.

Serve shrimp on steamed rice with the sauce drizzled over the top.

1 lb medium shrimp, peeled and de-veined

1 tbs canola oil

½ cup diced onions

¼ cup diced bell peppers

1 tbs minced garlic

1 tsp minced ginger

¼ cup white wine

1 tbs black bean sauce

¼ cup chicken broth

1 tbs soy sauce

¼ tsp cornstarch

Kosher salt & freshly ground pepper

Poached Sole over Buttered Pasta

This is an all time classic fish dish with a little added flair. And, it can't get any more basic to prepare. Substitute other fish for sole if desired as most fish work well with this recipe.

Cook pasta in a large pot of boiling, salted water according to package instructions. Drain, and set aside.

Melt 1 tablespoon of butter in a medium skillet. Once it melts, add scallions then place fish on top. Decrease heat to medium low, add wine, cover, and cook for 5 minutes. When fish is done, remove, and set aside. Reduce poaching liquid by ⅓, swirl in 1 tablespoon of butter, and season to taste with salt and pepper.

In another skillet, brown remaining butter. Add pasta, and season with salt and pepper. Once warm and coated with butter, add fish and combine. To serve, divide on two plates and drizzle with any extra sauce. If desired, garnish with fresh parsley and basil.

5 oz dried farfalle pasta

3 tbs butter, separated

¼ cup scallions, cut in rings

2—6 oz sole filets

½ cup white wine

Kosher salt & freshly ground pepper

Parsley

Basil

Spicy Ahi Tuna with Tropical Fruit Salsa

Tuna is best when cooked medium rare—think sushi. This dish is a perfect balance of sweet and hot with the molasses and Togarashi. The fruit salad balances it all out. Substitute mixed greens for rice as a variation.

Season tuna on all sides with salt and pepper, pour molasses over the top and rub, then sprinkle with Togarashi. Set aside.

In a bowl, combine fruit cocktail, tomatoes, and vinegar. Set aside.

Heat oil in a large skillet and add tuna. Cook for 1 minute on each side then brown remaining raw edges.

To serve, place a scoop of Rice Pilaf (recipe p. 110) in the center of each plate. Arrange tuna over the rice and spoon fruit salsa over the top.

2—6 oz ahi tuna filets

1 tbs molasses

**Sprinkle of Togarashi
(Japanese Powdered Chili Pepper)
or chili powder**

1 cup canned fruit cocktail

¼ cup diced tomatoes

1 tbs rice vinegar

1 tbs canola oil

Kosher salt & freshly ground pepper

Seafood

Poultry

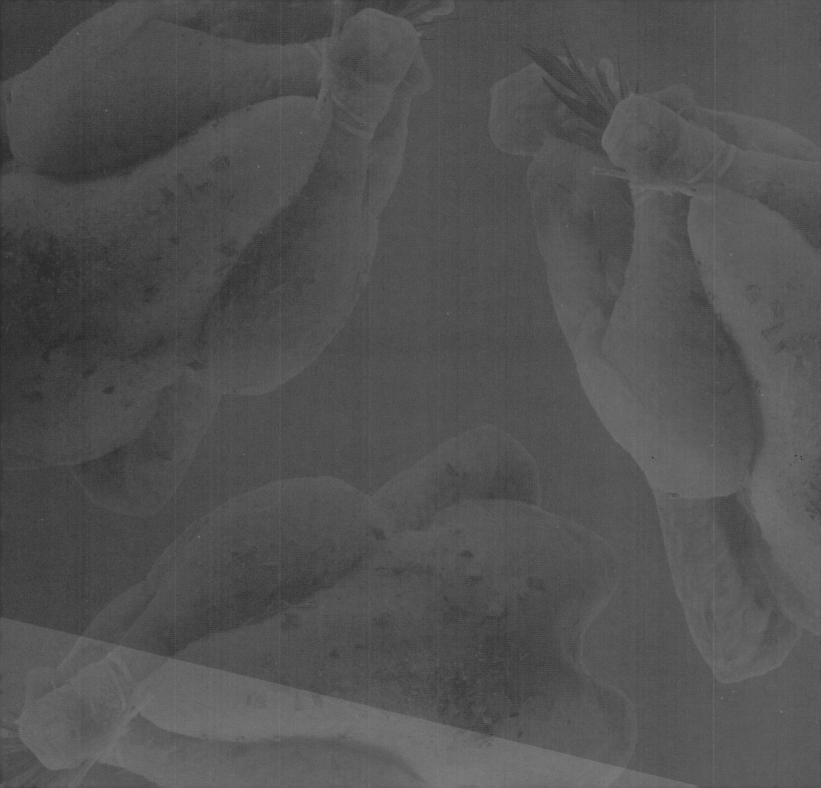

Turkey Meatloaf with Roasted Potatoes

Even though I make this dish well, Alberto, my line cook, makes it better. I give him full credit for this recipe. The leftovers make a delicious meatloaf sandwich the next day.

Pre-heat oven to 300°F.

In a mixing bowl, combine turkey, egg, parsley, carrots, tomatoes, breadcrumbs, cream, Worchester sauce, and chili sauce. Set aside.

Heat oil in a medium skillet. Add onions and cook for 1 minute. Remove onions from the pan, add to the turkey mixture, and season with salt and pepper. Thoroughly mix the ingredients together then remove from the bowl, place on a sheet pan, and form into a loaf, 7" long by 4" wide, by 2" high.

Season the potatoes with olive oil, salt, and pepper and arrange potatoes around the meatloaf. Cook in the oven for 30—40 minutes until done.

Slice meatloaf and arrange on two plates with potatoes.

1 lb ground turkey meat

1 egg, slightly beaten

1 tbs chopped parsley

¼ cup diced carrots

¼ cup diced tomatoes

⅓ cup dried breadcrumbs
(Panko preferred)

¼ cup heavy cream

1 tbs Worchester sauce

1 tbs sweet chili sauce

1 tbs canola oil

¼ cup diced onions

½ lb whole potatoes

1 tbs olive oil

Kosher salt & freshly ground pepper

Chicken Cacciatore

I'm not actually sure what Cacciatore means. But I do know that these are the ingredients that go into it. Even though it's an old school dish it holds up well today.

Pre-heat oven to 350°F.

Season chicken on all sides with salt and pepper. Heat oil in a medium, ovenproof skillet. Add chicken and cook for about 4 minutes on each side. Remove chicken from the pan and set aside.

Add mushroom, peppers, and zucchini to the same skillet. Let vegetables begin to caramelize, then add garlic and season with salt and pepper stirring occasionally. Add wine and reduce. Add tomato purée, and return chicken to the pan. Add broth and bake in the oven for 15–20 minutes.

To serve, place one piece of chicken on each plate. Spoon vegetables around the chicken and pour the sauce over the top. If desired, garnish with grated Parmagiano-Reggiano and chopped basil.

12 oz chicken pieces

1 tbs canola oil

1 cup sliced mushrooms

¼ cup diced red peppers

¼ cup diced zucchini

1 tbs minced garlic

½ cup red wine

⅓ cup tomato purée

¼ cup chicken broth

Kosher salt & freshly ground pepper

Chicken Fajitas

Using pre-cut vegetables makes this a turn key recipe. Since every ingredient has been prepared in advance, all you have to do is heat things up. Leave the assembly for your guests to do themselves.

In a mixing bowl, combine chicken, cumin, chili powder, 1 tablespoon oil, lemon juice, and garlic, and season with salt and pepper. Heat remaining oil in a skillet. Add chicken, onions, and peppers. Stir while chicken browns and onions and peppers soften, about 5–7 minutes. Be sure chicken is cooked all the way through. Place chicken and vegetables in a serving bowl and cover with foil to keep warm.

Heat tortillas in the same pan using tongs to flip. Once warm, remove tortillas from the pan and place on a serving platter. Serve salsa, sour cream, and guacamole on the side.

1 lb pre-cut chicken strips

½ tsp ground cumin

½ tsp chili powder

2 tbs canola oil, separated

1 tbs fresh lemon juice

1 tbs minced garlic

1 small onion, sliced into rings

1 red bell pepper, cut into strips

1 green pepper, cut into strips

1 pack flour tortillas

Kosher salt & freshly ground pepper

Turkey Scaloppini

Turkey is a good red meat alternative and can be substituted in place of veal. As with all scaloppini dishes, quick to prepare, tender on the palette, and delicious.

Season turkey breasts with salt and pepper then lightly flour both sides. Heat 1 tablespoon of oil and butter in a large skillet. Add turkey and reduce heat to medium. Lightly brown each side of turkey (about 2 minutes per side). Remove from pan and set aside.

Wipe out skillet with a paper towel and heat remaining oil. Add vegetables and season with salt and pepper. Add vermouth and demi-glace. Stir and cook until the vegetables are firm but done and season to taste with salt and pepper.

To serve, arrange turkey on warm plates and spoon vegetables on the side. Pour pan juices on top. If desired, serve over Polenta (recipe p. 114)

4 — ½" turkey breast slices

All-purpose flour

2 tbs canola oil, separated

1 tbs butter

1 cup frozen vegetable medley (eg: corn, carrots, green beans & peas)

¼ cup dry or sweet vermouth

¼ cup veal demi-glace

Kosher salt & freshly ground pepper

Stir-fry Chicken with Vegetables

Another dish made great thanks to Shmoo. Stir-fries are excellent utilization dishes. Chicken can be substituted for beef or pork, and the vegetables can vary depending on what's in season, on hand, or in the freezer.

Make the shmoo by mixing together soy sauce, oyster sauce, and sesame oil. Set aside.

Cut chicken into ½ inch cubes and season with salt and pepper. Heat oil in a large skillet. Add chicken and brown on all sides then add vegetables and season to taste with salt and pepper. Add wine and lower heat to medium. When the vegetables are almost done, add garlic. Cook for a few more minutes until vegetables are done but not mushy. Add shmoo and stir until thoroughly mixed.

Serve in even portions on two plates over Rice Pilaf (recipe p. 110) or steamed rice. If desired, garnish with chopped parsley and diced tomato.

Shmoo:

2 tbs soy sauce

2 tbs oyster sauce

2 tbs sesame oil

1 lb boneless, skinless chicken breasts

1 tbs canola oil

16 oz frozen Italian vegetable medley (green & yellow squash & red bell pepper)

¼ cup white wine

1 tbs minced garlic

Kosher salt & freshly ground pepper

Kung Pao Chicken

Kung Pao Chicken is a perennial favorite of Chinese cuisine. Most people have eaten it at least once and for many, it is the cornerstone of their order. This version is simple to prepare at home and doesn't require a wok.

Cut chicken into ½ inch cubes. In a mixing bowl, combine chicken, egg white, cornstarch, and season with salt and pepper.

Heat oil in a medium skillet. Add chicken and cook for 5 minutes stirring occasionally. Add peppers, ginger, scallions, sherry, Hoisin sauce, chili paste, and peanuts. Mix together and cook for 5 more minutes.

Serve Kung Pao Chicken on top of Rice Pilaf (recipe p. 110) or steamed white rice.

1 lb boneless, skinless chicken thighs

1 egg white, lightly beaten

2 tbs cornstarch

¼ cup canola oil

1 cup diced bell peppers

1 tsp minced ginger

½ cup chopped scallions (white parts)

¼ cup sherry

2 tbs Hoisin sauce

1 tbs fresh chili paste

½ cup chopped peanuts

Kosher salt & freshly ground pepper

Chicken Pot Pies

This is a delicious variation of a comfort food classic. The key to its success is the filling. The next time winter gets you down, serve these pot pies in front of a raging fire and you'll feel warm all over.

Pre-heat oven to 300°F

Unroll pie crust and place one ramekin upside down on crust. Cut crust around the ramekin leaving ½ inch of crust all the way around. Repeat this process for the second ramekin. Set aside.

Heat oil in a large skillet. Add chicken, onions, celery, vegetable medley, broth, and heavy cream, and season with salt and pepper. In a small bowl, mix together cornstarch and 1 tablespoon of cream. Once it's smooth, add to the skillet and stir until it thickens.

Spoon chicken mixture into the ramekins, and sprinkle parsley on top. Cover with crust, pinching in around the sides of the dish to seal. Place ramekins on a baking sheet and bake for about 30 minutes until crust is golden.

The pot pies will be very hot so place each ramekin on a plate before serving.

1 pack roll out pie crust

1 tbs canola oil

1 lb of chicken cut into ½ inch dices

½ cup diced onions

¼ cup diced celery

1 cup frozen vegetable medley, defrosted (corn, carrots, green beans & peas)

1 cup chicken broth

¼ cup heavy cream

1 tbs chopped parsley

¼ tsp cornstarch

Kosher salt & freshly ground pepper

2—4"–5" shallow ramekins

Lemon Chicken

If you like lemon and you like chicken, you won't be disappointed by this dish. Plus, it is simple, fast, and tasty.

Season chicken with salt and pepper, then dredge in flour, covering on all sides.

Heat oil in a large skillet, add chicken, and cook for 5 minutes. Add garlic and vegetable medley, and cook for 1–2 minutes. Add broth and lemon juice and cook for 5 more minutes. Remove chicken, cover with foil to keep warm, and set aside. Add cornstarch to the pan juices and bring to a boil while stirring until the sauce thickens.

Serve chicken on top of steamed rice and drizzle the sauce and vegetables over the top.

8 oz assorted chicken parts

Flour, enough to coat chicken

1 tbs canola oil

1 tbs minced garlic

16 oz frozen Italian vegetable medley (green & yellow squash & red bell pepper)

½ cup chicken broth

¼ cup lemon juice

1 lemon, sliced

1 tsp cornstarch

Kosher salt & freshly ground pepper

Roast Turkey with Sausage Stuffing

You'll appreciate dishes like this where the oven does the work, and frees you up to do other things. Be careful that you don't overcook the turkey.

Pre-heat oven to 300°F

Place turkey breast on a sheet pan, season liberally with salt and pepper, then rub with 1 tablespoon oil. Bake in the oven for 1 hour or until meat thermometer inserted into the thickest part reads 150°F. Remove, and let rest for 15 minutes.

While turkey is cooking, chop sausage into small dices. Heat oil in an ovenproof skillet, add sausage and cook for 2 minutes, until slightly brown. Add onions, scallions, bread-crumbs, and chicken broth. Stir. Just before removing turkey, place pan in the oven and bake for 15 minutes. Remove once ingredients begin to brown.

Slice turkey breast and arrange on plates. Serve stuffing on the side.

1—2 lb boneless turkey breast

2 tbs canola oil, separated

4 oz Louisiana hot sausages

½ cup diced onions

¼ cup chopped scallions

1 cup breadcrumbs

¼ cup chicken broth

Kosher salt & freshly ground pepper

Turkey Saltimbocca

This is a contemporary twist on an old-world veal dish. Because of the convenient packaging of turkey products, aside from being a combination of wonderful ingredients, this dish is easy and fast to prepare.

Pre-heat oven to 325°F.

Lay out two slices of turkey. Top each with a slice of proscuitto, followed by 4–5 sage leaves, then another slice of turkey. Sprinkle salt and pepper over the top and lightly flour both sides.

Heat 2 tablespoons of oil in a large skillet. Add turkey and reduce heat to medium-high. Lightly brown each side for 1 minute. Remove turkey and place onto a rimmed baking sheet. Bake in the oven for 5 minutes. Cover with foil and keep warm.

While turkey is in the oven, re-heat remaining oil in the skillet. Add onions and mushrooms and season with salt and pepper. Add garlic, wine, and demi-glace and bring to a boil. Remove from heat, add lemon juice, and season with salt and pepper.

Serve turkey with mushrooms and sauce over the top. If desired, make Risotto (recipe p. 108) to serve on the side. Garnish with capers.

4 turkey breast slices

2 slices of proscuitto

10 leaves of fresh sage

All-purpose flour

3 tbs canola oil, separated

2 tbs diced onions

2 cups sliced portabella mushrooms

1 tbs minced garlic

¼ cup white wine

¼ cup veal demi-glace

1 tbs lemon juice

Capers for garnish

Kosher salt & freshly ground pepper

Roasted Chicken and Vegetables

Everyone should know how to roast a chicken. Season it, place it in the oven, and make yourself busy doing other things while it cooks. When you return, it will be time to have dinner. A perfect oven-roasted chicken works for any occasion from a dinner party with friends to a mid-week family meal.

Pre-heat oven to 325°F.

Remove parts and excess fat from the opening of the chicken and rinse thoroughly. Liberally season the inside and outside with salt and pepper. Place a quartered apple, lemon, lime, or orange inside the cavity along with 2 cloves of garlic—peeled and roughly cut. Fold the wings under using toothpicks to secure, and tie the legs together with a rubber band or string.

Place chicken on a rimmed sheet pan. Drizzle with olive oil, and roast in the oven for 50 minutes.

In the meantime, rinse all vegetables. Cut leek lengthwise in half. Peel and cut carrot lengthwise and into quarters. Peel the bottom part of the asparagus. Cut potatoes into quarters or half depending on how large they are. Place vegetables into a mixing bowl; add garlic and olive oil, and season with salt and pepper. Mix until all vegetables are coated and set aside.

After 50 minutes, remove chicken from oven. Baste with pan drippings over the top and inside. Add vegetables in a single layer around the bird and return to the oven for 30 minutes or until done, turning the vegetables once.

Let chicken rest for 10 minutes then cut it into pieces and arrange on a large serving platter surrounded by vegetables.

1 whole 3–4 lb roasting chicken

1 apple, orange, lemon, or lime

2 cloves of garlic

Extra virgin olive oil

1 leek

1 carrot

5 asparagus spears

4 potatoes

1 tbs minced garlic

Kosher salt & freshly ground pepper

Chicken Soup

Whether chicken soup cures a cold or not may be debatable. It is true that chicken soup always warms the soul. This version tastes great and since its quick to prepare makes a good cold weather mid-week meal.

Wash chicken and season liberally with salt and pepper. Heat oil in a large stock pot. Add chicken and cook slightly. Add celery and onions, stir and cook for 5 minutes. Add broth, water, and bay leaves. Reduce heat, then cover and simmer for 20 minutes. Add vegetables and simmer for 10 minutes, then add noodles and cook until noodles reach their desired tenderness.

Serve in deep soup bowls with toasted, crusty bread on the side.

1 lb boneless chicken pieces, cut into 1 inch cubes

4 tbs canola oil

¼ cup diced celery

½ cup diced onions

8 cups chicken broth

8 cups water

2 bay leaves

2—10 oz packs frozen vegetable medley (e.g. corn, carrots, green beans & peas)

12 oz fine egg noodles

Kosher salt & freshly ground pepper

Beef,

Pork, & Lamb

Baby Back Ribs

With the exception of Dr. Hoggly Woggly's these are some of the tastiest ribs you will ever make. I like to use a honey-soy marinade, but barbecue sauce is easier and tastes good too. If you use barbecue sauce, I suggest Gayle's Original.

Pre-heat oven to 300°F.

In a large stock pot, add beer, water, garlic, bay leaves, peppercorns, salt, and ribs and bring to a boil. Reduce heat and simmer for 30–40 minutes. When the ribs begin to pull off the bone, remove, and place on a rimmed sheet pan. Season ribs to taste with salt and pepper and generously slather with barbecue sauce or marinade. Bake in the oven for 30 minutes, basting both sides every 10 minutes.

Remove, and slice ribs. Stack on one half of each plate with a scoop of Old Fashioned Potato Salad (recipe p. 112).

60 oz dark beer (5 bottles)

7½ cups water

2 garlic cloves, peeled

2 bay leaves

1 tsp black peppercorns

Kosher salt

1¼ lb rack of baby back ribs

Barbecue sauce or marinade

One Pot Beef Stew

The first time I attempted this dish I made it one-handed. My other hand had been burned and couldn't be used. The point is that if I can make this stew with one hand—you can certainly make it with two. And you will be glad you did. It is great tasting and simple.

Season beef generously with salt and pepper. Sprinkle flour on a flat plate and dredge beef through until completely covered. Heat oil in a large stock pot. Add beef and sear on all sides, turning with tongs. Remove when beef is evenly browned and set aside.

Add celery, carrots, onions, peas, and garlic to the same pot. Cook until soft, adding oil if necessary. Add wine and deglaze the bottom of the pot then reduce to the consistency of light syrup. Return beef, add broth, and bring to a boil. Reduce heat, cover, and simmer for 35—40 minutes. Add potatoes and cook for an additional 15 minutes, season with salt and pepper.

Divide the stew evenly into 2 deep bowls. Serve with warm bread on the side.

If desired, make an additional starch and serve the stew over that, i.e. Polenta (recipe p. 114), Rice Pilaf (recipe p. 110), couscous, or buttered noodles.

1 lb boneless beef stew meat

All-purpose flour

4 tbs canola oil

¼ cup diced celery

¼ cup diced carrots

½ cup diced onions

½ cup peas

2 tbs minced garlic

1 cup dry red wine

4 cups chicken broth

2 cups peeled and diced potatoes

Kosher salt & freshly ground pepper

Pork Tenderloin

This is the best rendition of pork. Like beef tenderloin, pork tenderloin dries out when overcooked—so be careful!

Pre-heat oven to 325°F.

Season pork with salt and pepper. Heat 1 tablespoon oil in a medium skillet. Add pork and cook 2–3 minutes per side until evenly browned. Remove, place on a rimmed baking sheet and bake in the oven for 8–10 minutes.

Heat remaining oil in a medium stock pot. Add onions and garlic; reduce heat to medium low and sauté 2–3 minutes. Turn heat to low, add demi-glace, bring to a boil, and season to taste with salt and pepper.

Serve pork on a platter with mixed greens. Drizzle the sauce over the top.

12 oz pork tenderloin

2 tbs canola oil, separated

¼ cup diced onions

1 tbs minced garlic

2 tbs veal demi-glace

Kosher salt & freshly ground pepper

Ginger Beef with Broccoli and Shmoo

My friend Rico and I created Shmoo when we worked together at the Nikko Hotel in Beverly Hills. This dish is straight forward, and the Shmoo makes it swing. I use a relatively inexpensive cut of meat to make this dish but it can be substituted with any cut, such as New York strip.

Make Shmoo: Mix together soy sauce, oyster sauce, and sesame oil. Cover, and set aside.

Heat oil in a medium skillet. Add beef, ginger, garlic, vegetables, and wine and reduce liquid by ½. Add shmoo and demi-glace. Toss together, season to taste with salt and pepper, and bring to a boil. Remove from heat and serve in bowls over Rice Pilaf (recipe p. 110).

Make extra Shmoo by using ¼ cup of each ingredient. What isn't used can be refrigerated.

Shmoo:

2 tbs soy sauce

2 tbs oyster sauce

2 tbs sesame oil

1 tbs canola oil

1 lb beef cut into ½ inch strips 4 inches long

1 tbs minced ginger

1 tbs minced garlic

⅓ cup sliced carrots

⅓ cup snow peas

⅓ cup broccoli florets

¼ cup white wine

¼ cup demi-glace

Kosher salt & freshly ground pepper

Pork Loin with Swiss Chard Ragout

This combination of pork, black-eyed peas, and Swiss chard melds together particularly well and makes a hearty winter meal. Pork chops can be substituted for the loin.

Pre-heat oven to 325°F.

Rinse pork, pat dry, and season with salt and pepper. Heat oil in a medium skillet. Add pork and cook on each side for 2–3 minutes until brown on all sides. Remove, and place on a rimmed baking sheet and bake in the oven for 20 minutes.

In the same hot skillet, add onions and garlic and sauté until slightly brown. Add wine to deglaze the pan and reduce by ½.

In the meantime, remove center core from Swiss chard, stack leaves on top of each other, roll up, and cut into ¼ inch ribbons. Add to the pan and cook until wilted. Add black-eyed peas, broth, and mustard powder. Bring to a boil, then lower heat and simmer, uncovered, until black-eyed peas are soft, about 20–25 minutes, and season to taste with salt and pepper.

Evenly divide the greens in the center of 2 plates. Top with sliced pork and pour the pan juices over the top.

2 6 oz boneless pork loins

1 tbs canola oil

½ cup diced onions

1 tsp minced garlic

¼ cup white wine, brandy, or Calvados

1 bunch Swiss chard

1 cup black-eyed peas

2 cups chicken broth

1 tsp mustard powder

Kosher salt & freshly ground pepper

Prime Rib, Roasted Potatoes, and Mushrooms

This is a classic and elegant recipe that always works well for a dinner party. Plus, it is simple to make and your guests will think you're a star in the kitchen.

Pre-heat oven to 325°F.

Generously season prime rib with salt and pepper. Heat oil in an ovenproof skillet. Add prime rib and sear for 3 minutes on each side. Remove from skillet and set aside.

Add potatoes to the skillet and coat with juices. Return prime rib to the skillet with the fat side in the air, and bake in the oven for 50 minutes. Remove, set prime rib aside, add mushrooms to the potatoes and stir in juices. Return prime rib to the skillet, season with salt and pepper, and return to the oven for 10 more minutes.

Slice the prime rib in half and put it in the center of a plate. Arrange mushrooms and potatoes around the side, and drizzle the juices over the top.

2 lb prime rib

1 tbs canola oil

½ lb fingerling or red new potatoes

12 oz cremini mushrooms

Kosher salt & freshly ground pepper

Rack of Lamb with Couscous and Spinach

Lamb is one of my favorite meats and the combination of the curry and spinach makes this one of my favorite dishes. Add more vegetables to the couscous if you desire.

Heat the broth in a large stock pot. Add curry powder and bring to a boil. Stir in couscous and cook according to package directions. Remove from heat, and season with salt and pepper. Cover, and set aside.

Pre-heat oven to 350°F.

Heat oil in a medium ovenproof skillet. Add lamb, bone side up and sear on all sides, using tongs to turn. (This doesn't take long and it will get smoky.) Once all sides are evenly seared, put the skillet in the oven and bake for 10–12 minutes. Remove, and set lamb aside.

Pour grease out of the skillet, and melt butter over medium heat. Add spinach, wilt, and season with salt and pepper. Remove and set aside in a bowl.

In the same skillet, add wine, and reduce by half. Add demi-glace, season with salt and pepper and bring to a boil.

Arrange the lamb on a platter surrounded by fluffy couscous. Pour the sauce over the top. Serve spinach on the side.

1 cup chicken broth

1 tbs curry powder

1 cup couscous

1 tbs canola oil

6-bone rack of lamb, Frenched (ask your butcher to do this for you)

1 tsp butter

6 oz baby spinach

¼ cup red wine

¼ cup veal demi-glace

1 tbs extra virgin olive oil

Kosher salt & freshly ground pepper

Veal Scaloppini, Spinach, and Gnocchi

This dish is so quick to make you'll be done eating it before the pan cools. As always, use the best quality meat available.

Season veal with salt and pepper. Sprinkle flour on a flat plate and dredge veal through until completely covered. Set aside.

Cook gnocchi in a large pot of boiling, salted water according to package instructions until they float. Drain, and set aside.

Heat 1 tablespoon of oil in a medium skillet. Add garlic and spinach and sauté until wilted and season with salt and pepper. Divide spinach onto two plates.

Wipe the skillet with a paper towel and add 1 more tablespoon of oil and butter. Once hot, add gnocchi. Season with salt and pepper and toss until gnocchi is evenly coated. Arrange gnocchi on top of the spinach in a pattern like the hours of a clock.

Wipe the skillet with a paper towel and add the remaining oil. Once oil is hot, add veal and cook for 10–15 seconds on each side—this is VERY fast! Place veal on top of spinach and gnocchi.

Return pan to heat and add wine. Reduce by half, then add demi-glace. Add salt and pepper to taste and bring to a boil. Remove from heat and drizzle over the veal.

4 — 3 oz thin slices of veal

All-purpose flour

8 oz gnocchi

3 tbs canola oil, separated

1 tsp minced garlic

1 cup baby spinach

2 tbs butter

¼ cup white wine

¼ cup veal demi-glace

Kosher salt & freshly ground pepper

Filet Mignon with a Blue Cheese Crouton

This is one of those elegant, architectural dishes, when you're cooking to impress. It sounds hard, but fear not. You don't need a cooking degree—just a little imagination. The combination of these ingredients makes for a very memorable meal.

Pre-heat oven to 350°F.

Generously season steaks with salt and pepper. Heat 1 tablespoon of oil in a medium skillet. Add the steaks and cook for 3–4 minutes, turn over, and cook 3–4 more minutes until both sides are evenly browned. Remove, and place on a rimmed baking sheet and bake in the oven for 15–20 minutes. Slice brioche in half; butter the topside and sprinkle with cheese. Place on a separate rimmed baking sheet, and put in oven to toast.

Pour grease out of the skillet. While still hot, add 1 more tablespoon oil and sauté mushrooms 3–4 minutes and season with salt and pepper. Remove from the skillet and arrange on 2 warm plates.

Re-heat the skillet and melt butter. Add spinach and season with salt and pepper. Wilt spinach slightly—be careful not to over cook—this happens in seconds. Remove spinach and arrange on top of mushrooms.

Wipe skillet with a paper towel and heat the remaining oil. Add onions and sauté until they have a little color then add vinegar and reduce by half. Add demi-glace, season to taste with salt and pepper, and bring to a boil.

Remove steaks and brioche from the oven. Place on top of the spinach and drizzle the sauce over the top.

2—8 oz beef tenderloin steaks

3 tbs canola oil, separated

2 brioche rolls (grocery deli section)

8 oz crumbled blue-cheese or Gorgonzola

8 portabella mushroom strips

1 tbs butter

16 oz baby spinach

¼ cup diced red onions

¼ cup sherry vinegar or balsamic vinegar

¼ cup veal demi-glace

Kosher salt & freshly ground pepper

Sautéed Liver

This was one of the dishes I was responsible for at the Odeon in New York. If you enjoy liver, and haven't tried making it at home, you'll appreciate this recipe for its simplicity and elegance. Use caution not to overcook.

Season the liver with salt and pepper on all sides. Sprinkle flour on a flat plate and dredge liver through until completely covered. Heat 1 tablespoon of oil in a medium skillet. Add liver and cook on each side for 2–3 minutes, until brown on both sides. Remove, cover with foil, and set aside.

Wipe skillet with a paper towel, add onions, and sauté until lightly browned. Add vinegar and reduce by half. Add demi-glace, bring to a boil, and season with salt and pepper.

Serve liver with sauce, lemon wedges, and chopped basil.

2—6 oz calves' livers (it may be more than 2 pieces)

1 tbs all-purpose flour

2 tbs canola oil, separated

½ cup diced red onions

½ cup sherry vinegar

¼ cup demi-glace

Kosher salt & freshly ground pepper

Lemon wedges

Chopped basil

Chili con Carne

Tenderloin of beef is what makes this dish special; beef stew meat will work fine too. Be careful with the chipotle peppers—they're hot! Have plenty of cold beer on hand in case your mouth ends up on fire.

Heat oil in a large stock pot. Add beef, and brown evenly on all sides. Add onions, bell peppers, garlic, cumin, chipotle peppers, tomatoes, and chicken broth and season. Stir together and bring to a simmer. Reduce heat to medium low, cover, and simmer for 30 minutes.

Ladle chili into deep bowls. If desired, serve with tortilla chips and a dollop of sour cream.

2 tbs canola oil

1 lb beef tenderloin cut into ½ inch cubes or stew meat

½ cup diced onions

¼ cup diced bell peppers

1 tbs minced garlic

1 tbs ground cumin

¼ cup chipotle peppers in Adobo sauce

½ cup crushed tomatoes

1½ cup chicken broth

Kosher salt & freshly ground pepper

Osso Buco, Orecchiette, and Vegetables

This is the quick version of a classic Italian dish. The longer and slower the Osso Buco cooks, the more tender and flavorful it will turn out. If you are in a rush, save this meal to prepare when time is not an issue.

Generously season osso buco with salt and pepper, and set aside.

Cook pasta in a large pot of boiling, salted water according to package instructions. Drain, return to the pot, add butter and parsley, toss, and set aside.

Heat 1 tablespoon of oil in a medium pot. Add osso buco and cook for 3–4 minutes on each side until evenly brown. Remove, and set aside.

Add onions, celery, and carrots to the same pot. If necessary, add a little more oil. Sauté for 1 minute. Add wine and deglaze the bottom of the pot, then reduce by half. Return osso buco to the pot and add enough stock to cover by 2/3. Increase heat to high, bring to a boil, reduce heat, cover, and simmer 30–40 minutes. When the meat is done, remove, and set aside.

Add 1 cup of the braising liquid to a small sauce pan and reduce by half. Add demi-glace, bring to a boil, and season to taste with salt and pepper.

Heat remaining oil in a medium skillet and stir pasta and Parmagiano-Reggiano together, season with salt and pepper.

To serve, divide the pasta on 2 warm plates. Place the osso buco on the side and drizzle the sauce over the top.

2—10 oz pieces osso buco

½ lb orecchiette pasta

2 tbs butter

1 tbs chopped Italian parsley

2 tbs canola oil, separated

½ cup diced onions

¼ cup diced celery

¼ cup diced carrots

¾ cup red wine

2 quarts beef or veal stock

¼ cup veal demi-glace

1 tbs freshly grated Parmigiano-Reggiano

Kosher salt & freshly ground pepper

Side Dishes

Fried Rice

This fried rice is better than any that you'll find in Chinatown. Add as many ingredients as you would like. Back in the day, I had an 18-ingredient fried rice on my menu. Come to think of it, that might have been a little overboard!

Make the shmoo: In a mixing bowl, combine soy sauce, oyster sauce, and sesame oil. Set aside.

Cook rice according to package directions. Set aside.

Heat oil in a medium pot. Add mushrooms, peppers, onions, assorted vegetables, garlic, and ginger and stir so that all ingredients are mixed together. While vegetables are still firm, add rice and shmoo. Mix well and continue cooking until vegetables are at desired tenderness.

Make fried rice a one-dish meal by adding cooked chicken, pork, beef, or seafood.

Shmoo:

3 tbs soy sauce

3 tbs oyster sauce

3 tbs sesame oil

Fried Rice:

1 cup rice

2 tbs canola oil

1 cup sliced mushrooms

¼ cup diced bell peppers

½ cup diced red onions

1 cup assorted stir fry vegetables (broccoli, carrots, & snow peas)

1 tbs minced garlic

1 tbs minced ginger

Kosher salt & freshly ground pepper

Risotto

Risotto started as peasant food. Now it's a menu staple in the best restaurants. Making risotto takes a little finesse but it's not that hard. Arborio rice is short and starchy and it cooks in stages. If you cook it too fast the inside will remain hard and the outside will be mushy. Be patient and serve al dente.

Rinse the rice. Heat the oil in a skillet. Add onions and cook until soft and translucent, then add rice and stir. Add wine to deglaze the pan and reduce until absorbed. Add 1 cup broth, and reduce heat to simmer. When all the liquid has been absorbed, add more broth ¼ cup at a time. Continue adding ¼ cup until liquid has been absorbed and risotto is al dente. When rice is done, add butter, stir in Parmagiano-Reggiano, and season with salt and pepper.

Serve risotto in deep pasta bowls. Garnish with chopped parsley, sage, or thyme.

1 cup Arborio rice

1 tbs canola oil

⅓ cup diced onions

⅓ cup white wine

At least 2 cups chicken broth

1 tbs butter

¼ cup freshly grated Parmagiano-Reggiano

Kosher salt & freshly ground pepper

Rice Pilaf

In one of my first jobs I was asked to make rice pilaf and it turned out terrible. This is a bulletproof recipe. Remember, rice needs to cook slowly in order to cook evenly and not be crunchy in the middle.

Melt 1 tablespoon of butter in a medium pot. Add onions, reduce heat to medium, and season with salt and pepper. Cook until onions are soft and translucent, about 3 minutes. Rinse rice and add, stirring to coat with butter and onions. Add broth; bring to a simmer, and cover. Turn heat as low as possible and cook until done—about 18 minutes. Once rice is done, stir in remaining butter and season to taste with salt and pepper.

2 tbs butter, separated

¼ cup diced onions

1 cup long grain rice

2 cups chicken broth

Kosher salt & freshly ground pepper

Crispy Noodle Cakes

Crispy Noodle Cakes are fun to make; they look impressive, and are good eating. Made properly, even the most discriminating guest will be dazzled.

Cook pasta in a large pot of boiling, salted water according to package instructions. Drain, then return to the pot, add chili paste, season with salt, and add 3 tablespoons oil. Mix together so that pasta is thoroughly coated.

Heat remaining oil in a large skillet and add half of the noodles. Keep heat at medium-low. Using the tip of the tongs, push down the edges of the noodles so there are no straggly pieces, forming a cake. After 6–8 minutes, check to see if the underside is golden and crunchy, and if it is, flip to the other side and cook until golden and crunchy. Remove the noodle cake and repeat the process with remaining noodles adding more oil if necessary.

To serve, cut the crispy noodle cake into 4 pieces and arrange decoratively on the plate with the tips facing out.

½ lb dry capellini or vermicelli pasta

1 tbs fresh ground chili paste

4 tbs canola oil, separated

Kosher salt & freshly ground pepper

Old Fashioned Potato Salad

This potato salad is picture perfect and worthy of being served in a pretty bowl on a tablecloth. Bring it to a summer picnic and reminisce about Grandma's potato salad from years ago.

Rinse potatoes, pat dry, and cut into quarters. Place in a stock pot. Cover with cold water and bring to a boil. Lower to simmer and cook until tender—check with a fork or knife blade. When done, drain, and set aside.

In large a mixing bowl, combine mayonnaise, mustard, and vinegar and season to taste with salt and pepper. Add hard-boiled egg, onions, and potatoes. Mix together then sprinkle with chives.

Transfer to a pretty serving bowl before serving.

1 lb red potatoes or fingerlings

½ cup mayonnaise

1 tbs mustard

2 tbs rice vinegar

1 hard boiled egg, coarsely chopped

¼ cup diced red onions

1 tsp chopped chives

Kosher salt & freshly ground pepper

Creamy Polenta

Polenta is a standard Italian dish that has recently become trés chic. It is versatile and will take on the flavor of any sauce served with it. Even without the infusion of a sauce from a main dish, this polenta recipe stands out with the rich combination of butter and Parmagiano-Reggiano.

Bring water in a medium stock pot to a boil. Reduce heat to low and whisk in cornmeal, stirring often so it doesn't stick. If polenta becomes too thick, add a little more water until it is smooth. After 10 minutes, add butter, Parmagiano-Reggiano, and season to taste with salt and pepper. Remove from the heat and serve immediately.

2 cups water

½ cup cornmeal

2 tbs butter

1 tbs freshly grated Parmagiano-Reggiano

Kosher salt & freshly ground pepper

Equipment Essentials

A complete set of equipment is as essential as a well-stocked pantry. This doesn't mean that you need to buy the most expensive or the fanciest gadgets. Following is a list of the necessary basics that will serve you time and again.

2—10" ovenproof Teflon pans
2—7" ovenproof Teflon pans
2—4 quart sauce pots
1—8 quart sauce pot

2—½ sheet pans
2—tin pie pans
1—set of stainless steel mixing bowls—1 quart, 2 quart, 4 quart

1—8" chef knife
2—tongs, heavy duty

2—wooden spoons
1—rubber silicone spatula
1—off-set turning spatula
1—slotted spoon
1—6–8" wire whisk
2—small cutting boards
1—set of measuring spoons
1—set of measuring cups

Japanese rice cooker

Essentials

Pantry Essentials

A well-stocked pantry and refrigerator is the key to being able to turn out meals quickly without having to take that extra trip to the store. Here's a list that I try to keep in stock at all times. Fresh ingredients should be purchased within a day or two of when you plan to make the recipe.

PANTRY:

Baking powder
Baking soda
Bay leaves
BBQ sauce
Beans (canned): white, lima
Breadcrumbs (Panko)
Cayenne pepper
Chicken broth
Chili flakes
Chili paste
Chili powder (Togarashi)
Chipotle peppers in adobo sauce
Cinnamon
Clam juice
Cornmeal
Cornstarch
Couscous
Cumin, ground
Curry powder
English muffins
Flour, all-purpose
Fruit cocktail
Hoisin sauce
Maple syrup
Molasses
Mustard: powder, grainy
Noodles, egg
Nutella®

Nutmeg
Nuts: peanuts, pine nuts, walnuts
Oil: canola, extra virgin olive, sesame
Oyster sauce
Pasta: capellini, fusilli, lasagna, rigatoni, spaghetti
Pepper: black, whole, ground
Potatoes: sweet, red, russet
Rice: Arborio, Calrose, long grain
Salt: kosher, sea
Sugar: powdered, granulated
Sun dried tomatoes
Tomatoes (canned): diced, crushed, whole
Vanilla bean extract
Vermouth: extra dry, sweet
Vinegar: balsamic, rice, sherry, white
Vodka
Wine: Madera, red, sherry, white
Worchester sauce

REFRIGERATOR:

Avocado
Basil, fresh
Butter: salted, unsalted
Carrots
Celery
Cheese: blue, cheddar, feta, mozzarella, Parmagiano-Reggiano, Swiss
Dill, fresh
Eggs, large

Garlic, fresh
Ginger, fresh
Lemons
Limes
Mango
Mayonnaise
Milk: whole, heavy cream
Mushrooms: sliced white, Portobello
Olives, Kalamata
Onions: red, scallions, yellow
Oregano, fresh
Parsley, Italian
Peppers : green, red, yellow
Sage, fresh
Sausage: Louisana hot, sweet Italian
Soy sauce
Spinach, pre-washed baby
Thyme, fresh
Tomatoes: Roma, cherry
Tortillas, flour
Turkey, sliced breast
Zucchini

FREEZER:

Chicken: boneless, skinless breasts, thighs, whole
Demi-Glace
Pasta: gnocchi, tortellini, ravioli
Vegetables: broccoli, corn, Italian vegetable medley, snow peas

Index

Express Aisle Gourmet

Copyright © 2006 by Silverback Books, Inc.

All rights reserved. No part of this book may be used or reproduced in any manner whatsoever without the prior written permission of the publisher.

Recipes and Text: Bill Dertouzos

Project Management and Editing: Lynda Zuber-Sassi

Design: Richard Garnas

Layout and Production: Patty Holden

Photography: StockFood

Printed in China

ISBN: 1-59637-056-4

Index